W9-BZP-380

A FALCON GUIDE®

Best Easy Day Hikes Series

best
easy
day hikes
Boulder

Tracy Salcedo

FALCON GUIDE®

GUILFORD, CONNECTICUT
HELENA, MONTANA

AN IMPRINT OF THE GLOBE PEQUOT PRESS

/A**FALCON**GUIDE®

Copyright © 2000 Morris Book Publishing, LLC
Previously published by Falcon Publishing, Inc.

Falcon and FalconGuide are registered trademarks of Morris Book Publishing, LLC.

Library of Congress Cataloging-in-Publication Data

Salcedo, Tracy.
  Best easy day hikes, Boulder / Tracy Salcedo.
    p. cm.
  ISBN-13: 978-1-56044-948-5
  ISBN-10: 1-56044-948-9
  1. Hiking--Colorado--Boulder Region--Guidebooks. 2. Boulder Region (Colo.)--Guidebooks. I. Title.
  GV199.42.C62 B6877 2000
  917.88'630434--dc21   00-021983

Manufactured in the United States of America
First Edition/Fifth Printing

Contents

Dedication
For my many cherished Colorado friends.

Acknowledgments

This book would not have been possible without the help of many knowledgeable people, including Pascale Fried of the Boulder County Open Space Department, Brent Wheeler of the City of Boulder Open Space Department, and Matt Claussen of the City of Boulder Mountain Parks Department, among others, for reviewing portions of the text. Thanks also to the Biehoffer family, the Charland family, George Meyers, the folks at Falcon Publishing, Sandy Weiner, Nancy Salcedo, Chris Salcedo, Erica Olsen, and finally, but most importantly, my sons, Jesse, Cruz, and Penn, and my partner and husband, Martin Chourré.

Map Legend

Interstate Highway/Freeway	(00)	Campground	▲
US Highway	(00)	Picnic Area	▭
State or Other Principal Road	(00) (000)	Building	■
Forest Road	416	Peak	9,782 ft.
Interstate Highway	⟹	Elevation	9,782 ft. ✕
Paved Road	⟹	River/Creek/Waterfall	
Gravel Road	⟹	Intermittent Stream	
Unimproved Road	====⟹	Marsh	↙
Trailhead	◯	Gate	•—•
Parking Area	Ⓟ	Bridge/Dam	⏝⏝
Main Trail/Route		Overlook/Point of Interest	◉
Main Trail/Route on Road		National Forest/Park Boundary	
Alternate/Secondary Trail/Route		Cliffs	
Alternate/Secondary Trail/Route on Road		Map Orientation	N
One Way Road	One Way	Scale	0 0.5 1 Miles
City	◯		

v

Overview Map of Boulder

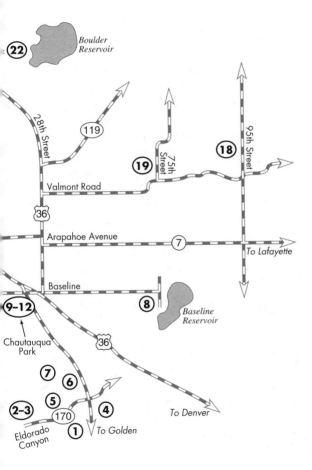

Ranking the Hikes

The following list ranks the hikes in this book from easiest to hardest.

Introduction

The Flatirons, monolithic slabs of smooth red rock thrusting toward the heavens, link the city of Boulder to the splendor of Colorado's Rocky Mountains, serving as a bridge between the human-altered landscape of the Front Range and the natural world of the high country. The rocks rise as though they aspire to something higher, and the day hikes in this guide offer the wanderer a chance to glimpse that higher ground.

Boulder is a fun town. Not only does it boast some of the hippest people, food, and shopping in the state, it is also surrounded by remarkable scenery unique to Colorado's Front Range. The stunning architecture of the Flatirons is a perfect example. Almost half of the hikes in this book wander in the shadows of these towering crags. By coupling these hikes with others on the prairie and in the high country, I have attempted to describe a diverse sampling of trails in the Boulder vicinity.

Each of the hikes herein, while varying in difficulty, terrain, and views, is within an hour's drive of the intersection of Broadway and Baseline Road in Boulder, just south of the heart of the city. Hikes are listed from south to north along the Front Range, and from east to west as you drive up canyons.

Easy, of course, is a relative term. Hikes in mountainous areas will inevitably involve climbing, and some would argue that no hike with inclines and declines is easy. To aid in the selection of a hike that suits particular needs and abili-

1

ties, I have ranked these from easiest to hardest. Keep in mind that even the steepest of these hikes can be made easy by hiking within your limits and resting when needed.

To determine how long it might take you to complete a hike, consider that on flat ground, most hikers average two miles per hour. Adjust that rate by the difficulty of the terrain and your level of fitness (subtract time if you're an aerobic animal and add time if you're hiking with kids), and you have a ballpark hiking duration. Add more time if you plan to picnic or participate in trailside activities like bird watching or photography.

This book represents an expansion of a guide I wrote more than five years ago for Chockstone Press, and in researching trails for this new book, I was again struck by the grandeur of the landscape in Boulder. These are blessed wildlands, and it is my sincere hope that those using this guidebook will be inspired to support the ongoing preservation efforts that have been so successful throughout the state. Hike on!

—*Tracy Salcedo*

Zero Impact

The trails that weave through parklands in and around Boulder are extremely popular, and accommodate an increasing number of visitors. We, as trail users and advocates, must be vigilant that our visits leave no lasting mark.

Trails can accommodate boundless travel if treated with respect. The book *Zero Impact* (Falcon Publishing) is a valuable resource for learning more about these principles.

The Falcon Zero-Impact Principles

- *Leave with everything you brought with you.*
- *Leave no sign of your visit.*
- *Leave the landscape as you found it.*

Litter is unsightly, and potentially dangerous to wildlife. Pack out all your own trash, as well as garbage left trailside by other hikers including biodegradable items like orange peels.

Use outhouses at trailheads or along the trail. There is seldom room or privacy along these routes for emergency backcountry practices. If you absolutely must go, carry a lightweight trowel so that you can bury your waste 6 to 8 inches deep, and pack out used toilet paper in a plastic bag. Be sure you relieve yourself at least 300 feet away from any wetland, creek, or lake, and well off any established trail.

Stay on established trails. Shortcutting and cutting switchbacks promote erosion. Select durable surfaces, like rocks, logs, or sandy areas, for resting spots. Do not approach or feed any wildlife. Be courteous by not making loud noises while hiking.

Please do not pick the flowers, gather plants, or collect insects, rocks, or other artifacts. Leave them for the next hiker to enjoy.

Do not feed the squirrels—they are best able to survive when they are self-reliant, and they are not likely to find snack food along the trail when winter comes.

Many of the trails described herein are also used by horseback riders and mountain bikers. Acquaint yourself with proper trail etiquette and be courteous.

Keep your impact to a minimum by taking only pictures and leaving only footprints. The wildlife and the people who will pass this way another day are thankful for your courtesy.

Play It Safe

Generally, hiking in this area is safe and fun. Still, there is much you can do to ensure each outing is enjoyable. Some suggestions follow, but by no means should this list be considered comprehensive. I encourage all hikers to verse themselves completely in the science of backcountry travel—it is knowledge worth having and it is easy to acquire. Written material on the subject is plentiful and easy to find through publishers such as Falcon, on the Internet, or through your area outdoors or sporting goods store.

Know the basics of first aid, including how to treat bleeding, bites and stings, and fractures, strains, or sprains. Few of these hikes are so remote that help can't be reached within a short time, but you'd be wise to carry and know how to use simple supplies, such as over-the-counter pain relievers, bandages, and ointments. Pack a first-aid kit on each excursion.

Familiarize yourself with the symptoms of altitude sickness, especially if you are visiting the area from a significantly lesser altitude—like sea level. If you or one of your party exhibits any symptom of this potentially fatal affliction, including headache, nausea, and unusual fatigue, head back down. The trail will still be there after you have acclimatized.

Know the symptoms of both cold- and heat-related conditions, including hypothermia and heat stroke. The best way to avoid these afflictions is to wear clothing appropriate to the weather conditions, drink lots of water, eat enough to keep the internal fire properly stoked, and keep a pace that is within your physical limits.

Be prepared for the vagaries of Colorado weather. It changes in a heartbeat. The sun can be brutal, so wear sunscreen. Afternoon and evening thunderstorms, while spectacular, harbor a host of potential hazards, including rain, hail, and lightning. Know how to protect yourself. And yes, snow may fall even in summer, so be on guard.

There are ways to deal with the more dangerous critters in the wilds, like mountain lions, bears, and rattlesnakes. Many parks post signs describing useful self-defense tactics should you encounter one of these beasties. Familiarize yourself with the proper etiquette.

Whether short and easy or long and strenuous, you will enjoy each of these hikes much more if you wear good socks and hiking boots. Carry a comfortable backpack loaded with ample water or sport drink, snacks and/or a lunch, and extra clothing, including a warm hat, gloves, and a jacket. Maps are not necessary, since these trails are short and well marked, but they are fun to have along. Bring whatever goodies interest you, like a camera, a manual to help you identify wildflowers, binoculars, or a good novel to curl up with on a warm rock.

1
FLATIRONS VISTA AND DOUDY DRAW TRAILS

Type of hike: Out-and-back.
Total distance: 6.8 miles.
Elevation gain: 480 feet.
Maps: USGS Eldorado Springs and Louisville; City of Boulder Open Space & Mountain Parks Lands Trails Map; Flatirons Vista/Doudy Draw brochure.
Jurisdiction: City of Boulder Open Space Department.
Facilities: There is ample parking, as well as restrooms, at the Doudy Draw Trailhead. Picnic and restroom facilities are available across Colorado 170 at the Mesa Trail South trailhead. Parking is also available at the Flatirons Vista Trailhead.
Finding the trailhead: From its intersection with Baseline Road, follow Broadway/Colorado 93 south for 4 miles to Eldorado Canyon Road (CO 170). Turn right (west), and follow CO 170 for 2 miles to the Doudy Draw Trailhead parking area, which is on the left (south). To reach the Flatirons Vista Trailhead, follow Broadway/CO 93 south from Baseline Road for 6.2 miles. The trailhead is well marked and is on the west side of the highway.

Key points:
0.0 Doudy Draw Trailhead.
0.3 Pass the picnic site.
1.5 Reach the fenceline and begin to climb out of the draw.

Flatirons Vista and Doudy Draw Trails

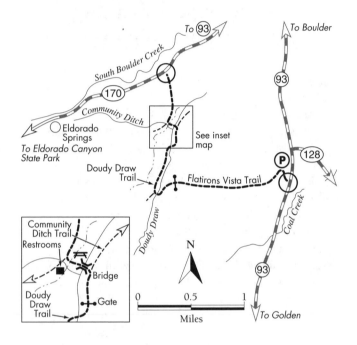

1.8 Arrive at the top of the mesa.
3.4 Reach the Flatirons Vista Trailhead.

The hike: The rolling meadowlands of Doudy Draw are a springtime delight. Purple penstemon and lupine, delicate white Sego lily, vivid yellow-flowering prickly pear, and scarlet Indian paintbrush appear in profusion in June and July;

pick up a field guide, plop down in a patch of prairie, and your knowledge of local flora will bloom with the wildlands.

The easy Doudy Draw Trail ends as a rather stiff climb onto a broad mesa that offers grand views westward into Eldorado Canyon. Some might consider the Flatirons Vista portion of the hike, atop the mesa, marred by the power line that traces its course, but walking westward along this path at sunset, when the mountains are backlit by the last of daylight and the plains glow rosy, is sublime. Both trail and power line are set in the shrinking tallgrass prairie that once dominated the high plains along Colorado's Front Range. Boulder County has been a leader in preserving this fading ecosystem, which sustains a number of grass and wildflower species.

The hike is described from Doudy Draw to Flatirons Vista, but can be hiked in either direction. Beginning at the Doudy Draw trailhead, pass through the gate at the southwest corner of the parking area, and follow the paved path south. At about 0.3 mile, you will pass a fenced-in picnic site, with restrooms, tucked in the shade of cottonwood trees. The pavement ends, and the trail splits. Take the left (southeast) fork, staying on the Doudy Draw and Community Ditch Trails.

Cross the stream, then climb to a second trail intersection. The Community Ditch Trail goes left (northeast); continue straight (south) on the Doudy Draw Trail, crossing the bridge over the ditch and then veering sharply south. No bicycles are permitted beyond this point.

The trail parallels a seasonal stream that runs below and to the right (west). At 0.8 mile, pass through a gate, being sure to close it behind you. The trail dips through a streamlet; the route is well marked with trail signs. Climb onto the west side of the stream, and pass under a power line with poles painted the same dusky pink as the rocks of the mountain backdrop.

Leave the power lines behind as the walls of the draw steepen and begin to close in. At about 1.5 miles, reach a fence line and trail intersection. Go left (east), on the Doudy Draw Trail.

Drop down and across the draw. Now comes the hard part: the trail climbs up the east face of the draw, where scruffy pines briefly shade the path. Climb a log staircase and pass a retaining wall, then round a switchback, and begin climbing north along the face, enjoying views of the Boulder Valley. Pass through another fence as you climb.

At 1.8 miles, reach a gate atop the mesa, where it will become abundantly clear how this section of trail earned the moniker Flatirons Vista. Follow the path as it arcs eastward, enjoying views of the high plains to the east. Pass through another gate into an open forest of stunted ponderosa pines that have likely been beaten down by the fierce winds that can howl out of the mountains. A mauve power line runs alongside the path.

The pines thin, then disappear as you approach yet another gate, again making sure to close it behind you. The trail drops over a grassy knoll, then curves southeast to the Flatirons Vista parking area at 3.4 miles.

Return as you came. Do not attempt to make a loop back to Doudy Draw along CO 93, as this would be both unsafe and unwise.

Option: You can do this hike in reverse by starting from the Flatirons Vista Trailhead. It's your choice…

2
RATTLESNAKE GULCH TRAIL

Type of hike: Out-and-back.
Total distance: 2.8 miles.
Elevation gain: 700 feet.
Maps: USGS Eldorado Springs; Eldorado Canyon State Park brochure.
Jurisdiction: Eldorado Canyon State Park.
Facilities: There is a small parking area and information kiosk at the trailhead; other amenities, including restrooms, are available at the visitor center, located west on the park road.
Finding the trailhead: From the intersection of Baseline Road and Broadway in Boulder, follow Broadway (Colorado 93) south for 4 miles to the stoplight at Eldorado Canyon Road (Colorado 170). Turn right (west) on CO 170 and follow it for 3.5 miles to the Eldorado Canyon State Park entrance and fee station. Pay the fee ($2 for walk-in traffic; $4 for automobiles). Drive up the entrance road for about 0.6 mile to the trailhead, which is on the left (south) side of the road.

Key points:
0.0 Trailhead.
0.2 Reach the Rattlesnake Gulch Trail.
0.9 Begin climbing switchbacks on the east-facing slope of the gulch.
1.4 Arrive at the ruins of the Crags Hotel.

Rattlesnake Gulch Trail
Eldorado Canyon Trail

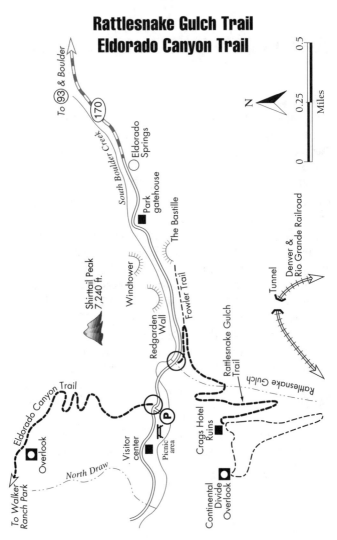

To 93 & Boulder

170

South Boulder Creek

Eldorado Springs

Park gatehouse

The Bastille

Shirttail Peak
7,240 ft.

Windtower

Redgarden Wall

Fowler Trail

Denver &
Rio Grande Railroad

Tunnel

Rattlesnake Gulch Trail

Rattlesnake Gulch

Eldorado Canyon Trail

Overlook

To Walker
Ranch Park

North Draw

Visitor center

Picnic area

P

Crags Hotel Ruins

Continental Divide Overlook

N

0   0.25   0.5
Miles

The hike: On a spectacular rock promontory, slowly succumbing to the forces of wind, snow, and sun, the brick skeleton of an oven overlooks the red rock walls of Eldorado Canyon. The oven, once mediocre amidst luxury, now lords over the remains of the Crags Hotel, which for a brief time was host to Colorado's wealthy and beautiful.

The Crags Hotel stood on this spot for only four years before it was destroyed by fire; an interpretive sign at the end of the trail describes its grandeur and demise. Metal and brick, potsherds that shine on one side with white or brown glazes, the foundations of the old funicular—these lonely remnants remain on the site, witnessing year-round views of the Continental Divide and Eldorado Canyon that once drew visitors by the hundreds to this site. Please leave all artifacts in place for the next hiker to enjoy.

The route follows the old "Crags Boulevard," which once led to the hotel. The grade, though steady, is relatively easy. This trail is shady and cool even on the warmest summer days, and it is spectacular in the afternoon and evening, when the setting sun stains the rocks of the canyon in shades of gold, red, and slate.

To begin, walk east on the broad gravel Fowler Trail, which parallels the park road and tumbling South Boulder Creek. At about 0.2 mile, just as views of the high plains appear between the rock walls at the canyon mouth, the Rattlesnake Gulch Trail breaks off to the right, switchbacking south, then west, and uphill into Rattlesnake Gulch.

As you climb, the trail curves south, away from Eldorado Canyon proper, and into the wooded draw. Talus slopes have achieved an angle of repose on either side of the path.

At about 0.7 mile, the trail curves through a flat, grassy area dotted with concrete foundations, then drops through the base of the gulch to the east-facing side. As the trail winds up along the slope, you will be treated to views of the steep spires and walls that make Eldorado Canyon a mecca for rock climbers.

At about 0.9 mile, you will reach the first switchback on the east-facing slope, and swing back to the south. The Denver and Rio Grande Railroad is chiseled into the mountainside above; if a train passes, the rumble of its engines wells up in the ravine, followed by the otherworldly whine of its wheels on the rails.

Go around another switchback; the trail is now guarded by a rustic fence, and great vistas both east and north ease any strain caused by the steady climb. As you near trail's end at 1.4 miles, the grade moderates, and the trail forks. Stay right (north) on the path that leads to a web of social trails that wind through the hotel ruins, which are perched on an exposed buttress of rock above the stunning Eldorado Canyon.

Once you have satisfied your inner archaeologist, return to the trailhead via the same route.

Option: If you choose, you can continue on the Rattlesnake Gulch Trail, which makes a 0.8 mile loop through the upper reaches of the gulch, and includes great views of the Continental Divide.

3
ELDORADO CANYON TRAIL

see map page 12

Type of hike: Out-and-back.
Total distance: About 4 miles.
Elevation gain: 1040 feet.
Maps: USGS Eldorado Springs; Eldorado Canyon State Park brochure.
Jurisdiction: Eldorado Canyon State Park.
Facilities: There is a small parking area and information kiosk at the trailhead; other amenities, including restrooms, are available at the visitor center, located west on the park road.
Finding the trailhead: From the intersection of Baseline Road and Broadway, take Broadway (Colorado 93) south for 4 miles to the stoplight at Eldorado Canyon Road (Colorado 170). Turn right (west) on CO 170 and follow it for 3.5 miles to the Eldorado Canyon State Park entrance and fee station. Pay the fee ($2 for walk-in traffic; $4 for automobiles) and park in the lot near the entrance. The hiking distance includes the short walk up the road to the trailhead.

Key points:
0.0 Trailhead.
0.4 Pass the Fowler Trailhead.
1.0 Switchbacks lead to a short descending traverse.
2.0 Reach the vista point.

The hike: This relatively strenuous hike is broken up by some of the most interesting scenery in the Boulder area. There is the commonplace—colorful wildflowers, magnificent trees, vistas of the Indian Peaks to the west—but it is the spider-people clinging to the impossibly steep rock overhanging South Boulder Creek that make the hike remarkable and different.

Eldorado Canyon has earned worldwide recognition for its spectacular rock faces, including the Bastille, the Whale's Tail, and Redgarden Wall. The multitude of colorfully clad rock climbers on the steep red rocks attests to its popularity. It is a mind-boggling, yet familiar distraction for many hikers, who may not have the nerve to ascend such monoliths but can understand the appeal of the challenge.

If you chose to begin this route near the park's entrance, you can pick the star of your own personal climbing show at the beginning of the hike, and mark that climber's progress at the hike's conclusion. If you don't want to catch the show, you can drive up the canyon to the Eldorado Canyon Trailhead, which begins just east of the visitor center.

From the parking area at the entrance station, head west up the main park road, passing beneath the Bastille on the south (left). The Whale's Tail, Redgarden Wall, and the Westside Ridge rise on the opposite (north) side of South Boulder Creek, which tumbles noisily over short waterfalls and through a diversion dam as you climb westward.

At about 0.4 mile, you will pass the Fowler Trailhead on the left (south). Continue west on the road. Cross the bridge that spans South Boulder Creek and go right (up and west) at the fork in the road to the Eldorado Canyon Trailhead at

0.5 mile. The trail departs on the right (north) side of the road, climbing stairs and two switchbacks into a draw.

Climb to a small saddle; beyond, the trail traverses from the east to the west side of the ridge, then through a forested gully onto the west-facing side of the draw. Views open south to the Denver and Rio Grande Railroad grade on the opposite wall of the canyon as the trail continues its rolling traverse.

At about the 1-mile mark, five switchbacks lead to a short, descending traverse. The trail soon climbs again, up four more switchbacks to a steep, open slope. Traverse through the meadowy terrain, enjoying views of the snow-capped Continental Divide to the west.

At about the 2-mile mark, you will arrive at a vista point at the western edge of the meadow, just before the trail begins to descend again. This is a great point for meditation or rest, and an ideal turnaround spot. Return as you came.

Option: The Eldorado Canyon Trail continues up and along the ridgetops above Eldorado Canyon for 4.5 miles, eventually leading into the trail systems of Boulder County's Walker Ranch Park, and the Crescent Meadows area of Eldorado Canyon State Park. If you are up for a longer hike of more moderate difficulty, carry on.

4
MARSHALL MESA TRAIL

Type of hike: Loop.
Total distance: About 2 miles.
Elevation gain: 180 feet.
Maps: USGS Louisville, City of Boulder Open Space & Mountain Parks Lands Trails Map.
Jurisdiction: City of Boulder Open Space Department.
Facilities: There is a small parking lot at the trailhead.
Finding the trailhead: From the intersection of Baseline Road and Broadway, travel 3.7 miles south on Broadway (Colorado 93) to Marshall Road (Colorado 170). Turn left (east) on Marshall Road, doubling back parallel to CO 93 to a stop sign. Turn right (east) at the stop sign, and continue on Marshall Road for 0.5 mile to the Marshall Mesa Trailhead, which is on the right (south) side of the roadway.

Key points:
0.0 Trailhead.
0.3 Pass the sandstone cliff and interpretive sign.
0.8 Reach the Community Ditch Trail.
1.5 Pass Marshall Lake.

The hike: For nearly 80 years, beginning in the mid-1800s, Marshall Mesa was the site of a huge coal mining operation. Walking through the peaceful prairie that thrives on the mesa today, such activity is difficult to imagine, but traces

Marshall Mesa Trail

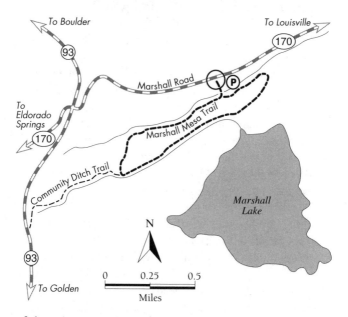

of the mines remain, and interpretive signs along the trail
describe the history—and the controversy—of the mining
operations.

The trail itself is pleasant and easy, winding up through
a blooming grassland to the Community Ditch, which you
follow to the shores of privately owned Marshall Lake. From
much of the trail, views spread west to the Flatirons, but are
curtailed to the east by the undulations of the high plains.
Much of the trail is shared with mountain bikers; be aware
of, and courteous to, these other trail users.

The trail begins at the southwest end of the parking lot. A small marsh lies along the outset of the path. Pass an interpretive sign, then cross the old railroad grade and climb a switchback up to a bridge across the ditch. At the trail intersection, stay right (southwest) on the Marshall Mesa Trail.

The path climbs west through the wildflower-littered grassland. At about the 0.3-mile mark, the trail enters an area of sparse ponderosa and skunkbrush. The trail curves into a gully highlighted by a stained sandstone cliff, where an interpretive sign discusses the geology of the area. Climb above the gully to the top of the mesa and an intersection with a social trail that leads right (west). An interpretive sign at this point describes the underground coal fires that plagued the area. Continue straight (south) on the main trail.

At about 0.8 mile, pass through a gate, ignoring a social trail that leads left (east), and walk uphill for 100 yards to the Community Ditch Trail. Go left (east) on the Community Ditch Trail. At about 1.5 miles, the ditch bends south into Marshall Lake. A trail leads up and right (south) to a lake overlook; there is no trespassing along the lakeshore.

From here, you can return as you came, or continue east on the Community Ditch Trail. The wide doubletrack continues for 0.3 mile beyond the lake's inlet to a broad, lazy switchback, which loops to the left (north). Where signs indicate closed social trails that continue east, stay on the main route, which bends west and passes an interpretive sign about violent strikes in the coal mines. The trail drops to parallel the lower ditch, passes the last interpretive sign describing the coal mining process, then hitches up with the Marshall Mesa Trail above the bridge at the trailhead.

5
TOWHEE AND HOMESTEAD TRAILS

Type of hike: Loop.
Total distance: 1.9 miles.
Elevation gain: 360 feet.
Maps: USGS Eldorado Springs; City of Boulder Open Space & Mountain Parks Lands Trails Map; City of Boulder Open Space Department's Mesa Trail South brochure.
Jurisdiction: City of Boulder Open Space Department.
Facilities: There is a parking lot and an informational kiosk at the trailhead, as well as restrooms and picnic tables. Dogs must be on leash on the Towhee section of this hike.
Finding the trailhead: From the intersection of Broadway and Baseline Road, follow Broadway/Colorado 93 south for 4 miles to Eldorado Canyon Road (Colorado 170). Turn right (west), and follow CO 170 for 2 miles to the Mesa Trail South Trailhead parking area, which is on the right (north).

Key points:
0.0 Trailhead.
0.2 Head west on the Towhee Trail.
0.6 Drop into the gully.
1.2 Reach the intersection of the Homestead and Towhee Trails.
1.6 Hike down the staircase toward the homestead.

Towhee and Homestead Trails

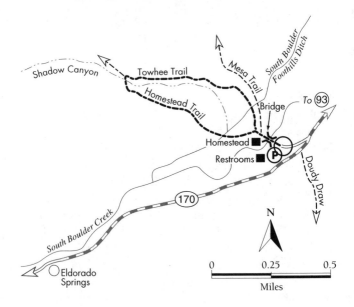

The hike: This gentle loop captures the best of Colorado's foothills in a single sweep. From tumbling nourishment provided to the prairie by South Boulder Creek, to the rustic shelter of the historic Doudy-Debacker-Dunn House, to the wildness of the overgrown thickets of lower Shadow Canyon, the trail encapsulates both the natural and manmade history of the area. The red rock portals of Eldorado Canyon, which rise to the west, give this adventure a distinctive Boulder twist.

The trail begins in the northeast corner of the parking area, on the signed Mesa Trail. Cross a small bridge spanning the Davidson Ditch; the trail forks immediately, with the left (west) fork making a short detour around a small meadow to the shores of South Boulder Creek. Continue straight (north) on the wider Mesa Trail, where a wooden bridge crosses South Boulder Creek.

The picturesque Doudy-Debacker-Dunn House, two stories of wood, stone, and homesteading history, stands on the west side of the trail about 100 yards from the north bank of the creek. Named for its three owners and residents, you can read an interpretive sign about the house and surrounding ranch at this point, or wait until you pass it again at the trail's end.

To continue, hike northwest to the intersection of the Mesa and Homestead Trails. Turn left (west) on the Homestead Trail, walk about 50 yards, then turn right (northwest) on the Towhee Trail at 0.2 mile. The narrow footpath leads up past a stately cottonwood toward the Flatirons and distinctive Devils Thumb.

The Towhee Trail cuts through one of the rustic rock walls that weave through the ranch, then over a culvert, as it continues its gentle ascent toward Shadow Canyon. The surrounding meadows, alive with birdsong, are studded with wildflowers and red sandstone boulders. A thicket of willow and other shrubs crowds the trail at 0.3 mile, nurtured by a murmuring seasonal stream. A rustic log staircase leads to an easy streambed crossing, then the trail roughly parallels the waterway as it traverses the south-facing slope of the narrowing gulch.

The path grows rougher as it ascends to the west. At 0.6 mile, the trail forks; take the left (lower) branch, which arcs west into the gully. At about 0.7 mile, you will drop into the heart of the draw, and trace the small stream's route up through the riparian zone, enjoying a brief respite before the climbing resumes. Stairs aid in the ascent.

The first evergreens shade the trail as you approach the Towhee and Homestead Trail intersection at 1.2 miles. Take the time to cool your feet in the tinkling stream before you turn left (southeast), cross the creek, pass the trail sign, and begin the return leg of the loop on the Homestead Trail.

A brief climb leads to a pine-dotted ridgetop on the south side of the draw. As you begin to descend at about 1.3 miles, views of the high plains open to the east, the flat green sweep broken only by gullies at the base of the mesa and silvery clusters of civilization. The trail follows the crest of the ridge through alternating meadows and glades. Log steps break up the rocky descent.

At about 1.6 miles, the trail dives south off the ridge via a winding staircase that drops toward the highway snaking into Eldorado Springs. By the time you reach the second flight of the staircase, the trail has arced eastward, and the homestead is in view.

At 1.8 miles, pass the Homestead Trail sign at the trail intersection, and go left (east) toward the house. The spur trail on the right (south) leads to the shore of South Boulder Creek. Cottonwoods and the creek itself cool the final stretch of the hike. At the next trail intersection, go left (northeast) to the house and Mesa Trail, then retrace your steps back to the trailhead.

6
BIG BLUESTEM AND SOUTH BOULDER CREEK TRAILS

Type of hike: Loop.
Total distance: 4.6 miles.
Elevation gain: 380 feet.
Maps: USGS Louisville and Eldorado Springs; City of Boulder Open Space Mesa Trail South Trailhead brochure; Colorado Mountain Club Boulder Group's Trail Map to Boulder Mountain Parks and Nearby Open Space; City of Boulder Open Space & Mountain Parks Lands Trails Map.
Jurisdiction: City of Boulder Open Space Department.
Facilities: There is ample parking and a restroom at the trailhead. Please heed seasonal leash requirements for dogs.
Finding the trailhead: To reach the South Boulder Creek Trailhead from the intersection of Broadway and Baseline Road, follow Broadway (Colorado 93) south for 3.2 miles to Thomas Lane. Turn right (west) on Thomas Lane; the parking area is obvious.

Key points:
0.0 Trailhead.
2.0 Reach the Mesa Trail intersection.
2.3 Head north on the Big Bluestem Trail.

The hike: In late spring and summer, you will hardly be able to see the big bluestem grass for which a portion of this loop

Big Bluestem and South Boulder Creek Trails

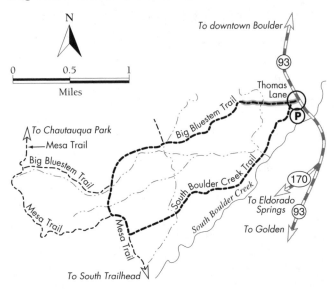

is named because the wildflowers will be too thick. You will find penstemon, lupine, Indian paintbrush, and sego lily along the route, among others; bring along a wildflower guide, or better yet, a botanist friend. It will be educational.

If you can peel your eyes away from the flowers, they'll without doubt be drawn upward to the red ramparts of the Flatirons, which rise to the west of the trail. The path climbs gently toward their base, but veers back east before you enter the forest that darkens their lower slopes.

From the trailhead, follow the wide roadbed south for about 0.1 mile, passing the Lafayette Water Plant, to where the South

Boulder Creek Trail branches to the right (southwest) and becomes a footpath (there is a sign here). The trail merges with the roadbed again; pass through a gate as you continue south along the South Boulder Creek corridor.

You will pass through three more gates before the trail arcs to the west and begins to climb toward the mountains. Always close all gates behind you. Log steps lead through the meadow grasses to another gate. Beyond this, the trail continues its steepening (but never truly steep) climb.

As you ascend, you will cross a small footbridge over a seasonal stream, and pass through yet another gate. At 2.0 miles, the South Boulder Creek Trail dead-ends at the Mesa Trail. Turn right (north) on the Mesa Trail, and follow it for 0.3 mile to the Big Bluestem Trail. This is, perhaps, the steepest section of the route; it is all downhill from here.

Turn right (northeast) onto the Big Bluestem Trail, which loops down across the bed of a seasonal stream (watch for poison ivy here), then climbs stairs to a trail intersection. The left (west) branch of the Big Bluestem Trail leads back to the Mesa Trail; turn right (northeast) to loop back to the trailhead, crossing another little streamlet and passing a gate.

The Big Bluestem Trail widens from singletrack to doubletrack to roadbed as it descends through the prairie. At about 3.3 miles, a spur trail leads north toward a forested rise and a fence; stay right (east) on the Big Bluestem Trail.

At about 4 miles, you will pass through yet another gate, skirting an old corral that lies to the north of the route. The trail veers left (north), then east at the fenceline, and leads through a gate onto Thomas Lane. Follow the road, passing private homes, back to the trailhead parking area.

7
WALTER ORR ROBERTS NATURE TRAIL

Type of hike: Loop.
Total distance: 0.4 mile.
Elevation gain: 74 feet.
Maps: USGS Eldorado Springs.
Jurisdiction: National Center for Atmospheric Research.
Facilities: There is ample parking in the National Center for Atmospheric Research (NCAR) parking lot. Restrooms are available in the research center. NCAR also offers tours of its Mesa Laboratory facility, and there are fascinating displays of weather phenomena in its entry halls.
Finding the trailhead: From the intersection of Broadway and Baseline Road, head south on Broadway for 1.2 miles to Table Mesa Drive. Turn right (west) on Table Mesa Boulevard, and go 2.4 miles to where the road ends in the NCAR parking lot. The trailhead is on the northwest side of the building.

Key points:
0.0 Trailhead.
0.2 Reach the west end of the loop.

The hike: This sweet little loop, also called the Walter Orr Roberts Weather Trail, boasts wonderful interpretive signs

Walter Orr Roberts Nature Trail

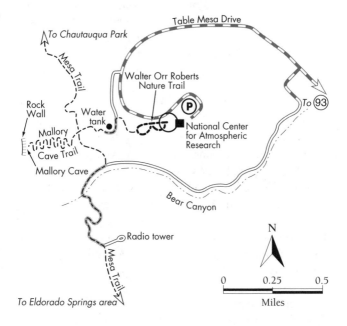

and gorgeous views, making it a must for families with young children and anyone interested in the weather that affects the Front Range. It also can serve as the perfect introduction to foothills hiking for visitors to the area, and is accessible to persons with disabilities. In addition, it links to the more lengthy Mesa Trail and the wonderful trail system that branches off from this artery.

Eleven viewpoints with interpretive signs line the figure-eight path, discussing the sometimes fierce and always interesting weather along the Front Range, including Denver's infamous "Brown Cloud," chinook winds, snow, flooding, and thunderstorms. To the east, beyond the striking architecture of the NCAR building, the high plains present a panorama shimmering with the silver of development and the gold and green of prairie grasses. To the west, the foothills rise to the Flatirons, which in turn extend to the high peaks of the Continental Divide, where much of the weather that sweeps over Boulder develops.

Pick your path along the interpretive route; the broad path winds uphill to the west for about 0.2 mile, then loops back to the trailhead, and features several benches for rest and contemplation. A short intersecting path runs between the two main arms of the trail, creating the figure eight. Once you complete the trail, you may want to visit NCAR's Mesa Laboratory, where you will find a number of interesting displays.

Options: At the west end of the nature trail, a sign points west toward the Mesa Trail. This path makes a nice, short addition to the nature trail, and links to the extensive trail system along the base of the Flatirons.

The path begins by heading down and south on a switchbacking rock staircase to a traverse of the south-facing slope of the Table Mesa. Remain on the main path as you circle the mesa, ignoring side trails that branch off to the left (west). Drop through a saddle, then head up into the trees, climbing switchbacks and rustic stairs to a large weathered water tank. Go left (west) on the tank service road to the trail, which resumes behind (on the west side of) the water tank, narrows to singletrack, and then drops to the Mesa Trail.

From the Mesa Trail intersection, you have a multitude of choices. You can head right (north) toward the wonderful trails in Chautauqua Park, or left (south) toward Eldorado Canyon. Or, you can go directly west onto the difficult Mallory Cave Trail, which begins with deceptive ease, wandering up through alternating meadow and forest into the wrinkles of the Flat-irons. When the trail becomes hard, it becomes extremely hard, climbing more than 20 switchbacks and a series of rustic stone staircases toward Mallory Cave. A final rock scramble of more than 100 feet up an exposed crease in a red rock slab leads to the cave itself; this is an adventure for only the hardiest and most experienced of hikers.

8
SOUTH BOULDER CREEK: BOBOLINK NATURE TRAIL

Type of hike: Out-and-back.
Total distance: 2.6 miles.
Elevation gain: Minimal.
Maps: USGS Louisville, City of Boulder Open Space & Mountain Parks Lands Trails Map.
Jurisdiction: City of Boulder Open Space Department.
Facilities: There is ample parking at the trailhead. Interpretive signs line the first portion of the trail.
Finding the trailhead: From the intersection of Baseline and Broadway, follow Baseline east for 9.9 miles to the trailhead parking area. The parking area is on the right (south) side of the road about 50 yards west of Baseline's intersection with Cherryvale.

Key points:
0.0 Trailhead.
0.5 Reach the end of the nature trail.
1.2 Arrive at the tunnel under South Boulder Road.

The hike: Gurgling and sparkling, with its bower of stately cottonwoods and lush border of wildflowers and shrubbery, South Boulder Creek is the soul of this hike. Interpretive signs along the first half of the trail describe the diversity of riparian and prairie habitats, and the importance of water

South Boulder Creek: Bobolink Nature Trail

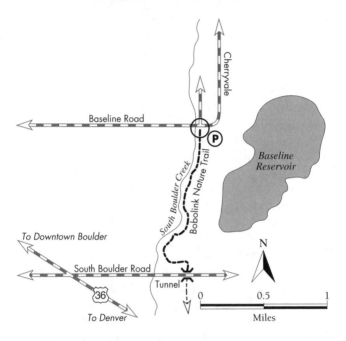

conservation. With development encroaching on this narrow strip of parkland, the importance of its preservation, and the health of the ecosystems it supports, is all the more poignant. Much of this area was recently designated a natural area by the State of Colorado in recognition of the diversity of its plants and animals.

The trail, which is easy and well maintained, is extremely popular with hikers, trail runners, and dog walkers; dogs must be under voice and sight control and are prohibited from the trail south of South Boulder Road. Streamside rock benches are great for contemplating the shimmering water and the mountain backdrop that rises to the west.

The trail begins in the southwest corner of the parking area. It begins as an easy meander along the creek, with several footpaths that lead to the waterside. At about 0.4 mile, cross a bridge spanning a tributary stream; here, the dirt trail briefly parallels the paved bike path, then splits again. The side-by-side trail setup recognizes that, though equally valid, cycling and hiking are not necessarily compatible.

The creek is blocked by a diversion dam; beyond, a gate marks the end of the nature trail at 0.5 mile. If you choose, you can continue south, crossing the bike path where the trails merge again. Beyond this point, hikers and cyclists must share the same path.

Continue southwest on a streamside meander, passing an old, gray farm structure. At about 1.2 miles, as you approach South Boulder Road, you will cross a silver culvert; the trail curves east, shadowing the road toward Baseline Reservoir, to a tunnel that leads under the road. Turn back before the tunnel—or earlier, if you do not want to hear the roadside noise—and retrace your steps to the trailhead.

Option: The trail continues south along South Boulder Creek to Marshall Road. Dogs are prohibited on this section of trail.

9
ENCHANTED MESA AND McCLINTOCK NATURE TRAILS

Type of hike: Loop.
Total distance: 2 miles.
Elevation gain: 440 feet.
Maps: USGS Eldorado Springs; Colorado Mountain Club Boulder Group's Trail Map to Boulder Mountain Parks and Nearby Open Space; City of Boulder Open Space & Mountain Parks Lands Trails Map; City of Boulder Mountain Parks Circle Hikes brochure.
Jurisdiction: Chautauqua Park/City of Boulder Mountain Parks.
Facilities: In addition to parking, there are picnic tables at the trailhead.
Finding the trailhead: Follow Baseline Road west for 0.8 mile from its intersection with Broadway. Go left (south) onto 12th Street for 0.1 mile to Columbine. Go right for 0.2 mile on Columbine to the parking lot for the Chautauqua Auditorium. Park in the auditorium lot; the trail begins on the southeast side of the building.

Key points:
0.0 Trailhead.
0.2 Pass the covered reservoir.
1.2 Reach the trail intersection by the picnic rock.
1.8 Return to the Enchanted Mesa Trail.

Enchanted Mesa and McClintock Nature Trails, Bluebell Mesa Loop, and Royal Arch Trail

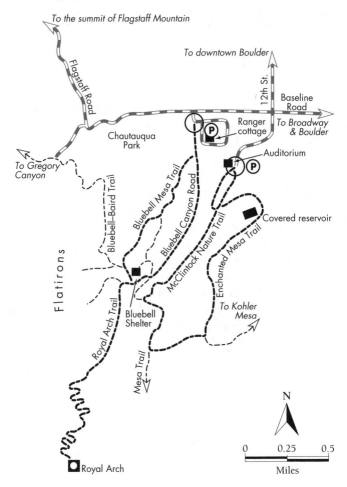

To the summit of Flagstaff Mountain

To downtown Boulder

Flagstaff Road

12th St.

Baseline Road

To Broadway & Boulder

Chautauqua Park

Ranger cottage

Auditorium

To Gregory Canyon

Bluebell–Baird Trail

Bluebell Mesa Trail

Bluebell Canyon Road

McClintock Nature Trail

Enchanted Mesa Trail

Covered reservoir

Flatirons

Royal Arch Trail

Bluebell Shelter

To Kohler Mesa

Mesa Trail

N

Royal Arch

0   0.25   0.5

Miles

The hike: The Enchanted Mesa and McClintock Nature Trails combine to make an easy, well-maintained loop (spiced with a few steep sections, both up and down) that meanders through a lovely woodland and features great views of the high plains and the famous Flatirons.

The loop is ideal for young ones, given its short length and relatively easy inclines. For those who need a little coaxing, promise a treat on a picnic rock in the woods at the apex of the trail. It is all downhill from there, and the latter part of the hike follows an interpretive trail with signs describing area flora and fauna.

Start by climbing the service road that serves as the Enchanted Mesa Trail, which leads south toward the Flatirons, gently ascending through an arbor of trees. After less than 0.1 mile, the trail curves left (eastward) and forks. Stay left (east) on the road marked Enchanted Mesa.

At about 0.2 mile, pass a short access road that leads to the base of a covered reservoir on the right (south) side of the trail. Curve westward, staying on the service road/Enchanted Mesa Trail as it meanders lazily through an open pine woodland.

At 1.2 miles, you will reach the intersection of the Enchanted Mesa and Mesa Trails. This is the high point of the loop, and a perfect place to take a break. Go ahead, have that candy bar.

To continue, go right (north) on the Mesa Trail, which begins a gentle descent through the pine forest. When the Mesa Trail intersects the McClintock Nature Trail, go right (north) on the McClintock Nature Trail.

Descend some steps to a flat area, then follow the trail along the side of a gully. Ignore a narrow spur trail that breaks off to the right (east), staying left (northeast and down).

At about 1.8 miles, reach the Enchanted Mesa Trail at the stone bridge you passed near the outset of the trail. The continuation of the McClintock Nature Trail is about 20 feet to the east of the stone bridge. Continue creekside on the McClintock path to the fork with a spur trail at a big rock. Go left (west) over the footbridge and climb up and out of the creek basin into the parking area.

10
BLUEBELL MESA LOOP

see map page 36

Type of hike: Loop.
Total distance: About 1 mile.
Elevation gain: 520 feet.
Maps: USGS Eldorado Springs; Colorado Mountain Club Boulder Group's Trail Map to Boulder Mountain Parks and Nearby Open Space; City of Boulder Open Space & Mountain Parks Lands Trails Map.
Jurisdiction: Chautauqua Park/City of Boulder Mountain Parks.
Facilities: There is a large parking area at the Chautauqua Park trailhead, but on busy summer days, this lot can be full. If this is the case, you can park along the south side of Baseline Road or along neighborhood streets. Restrooms, as well as information and trail maps, are located at the ranger cottage.
Finding the trailhead: From its intersection with Broadway, go west on Baseline Road for 1.1 miles to the entrance to Chautauqua Park, which is on the left (south) side of the road.

Key points:
0.0 Trailhead.
0.4 Pass the Mesa Trail.
0.5 Reach the Bluebell Shelter.

The hike: This scenic and popular path attracts nature lovers, hikers and runners with a passion for a workout, and couples walking hand-in-hand through spectacular wildflowers. The route winds through a beautiful meadow that sweeps down from the base of the First Flatiron; springtime in the meadow brings forth a bevy of colorful blooms that rivals any display along the Front Range. From the Bluebell Canyon Road, great views of the majestic Flatirons form a stunning backdrop for the meadow.

To begin, pass through the parking area via the paved Bluebell Canyon Road, which climbs southward adjacent to Chautauqua's cottages. Leave the houses behind as the path curves west and offers stunning views of the Flatirons.

At about 0.4 mile, reach the Mesa Trailhead and a restroom. Continue on the road past the restroom. The road forks at the Bluebell Shelter sign, and makes a loop up and around the shelter. Bear to the left (southwest), heading up the road toward the Royal Arch Trail and the Bluebell Shelter. Take the Bluebell-Baird Trail, which departs from the left (west) side of the Bluebell Shelter; follow this to its intersection with the Bluebell Mesa Trail at 0.5 mile. Go right (northeast) and down on the Bluebell Mesa Trail, which begins in an open ponderosa parkland.

Reach the Bluebell Shelter Trail crossing, and enjoy the great views to the east. Stay left (northeast) on Bluebell Mesa Trail as it descends into the meadow. Log stairs carved into the hillside drop through the grasses and wildflowers. Please do not pick or remove the wildflowers, as it is prohibited. Stay on the trail, which continues to descend, though not steeply, to Bluebell Canyon Road. The parking area is not more than 0.1 mile to the north along the Bluebell Canyon Road.

11
ROYAL ARCH TRAIL

see map page 36

Type of hike: Out-and-back.
Total distance: 3 miles.
Elevation gain: 1100 feet.
Maps: USGS Eldorado Springs; Colorado Mountain Club Boulder Group's Trail Map to Boulder Mountain Parks and Nearby Open Space; City of Boulder Open Space & Mountain Parks Lands Trails Map.
Jurisdiction: Chautauqua Park/City of Boulder Mountain Parks.
Facilities: There is a large parking area at the trailhead, but on busy summer days, this lot can be full. If this is the case, you can park along Baseline Road or along neighborhood streets. Restrooms, as well as information and trail maps, are located at the ranger cottage.
Finding the trailhead: From its intersection with Broadway, go west on Baseline Road for 1.1 miles to the well-marked entrance to Chautauqua Park, which is on the left (south) side of the road.

Key points:
0.0 Trailhead.
0.5 Reach the Royal Arch Trail.
0.8 Pass the Third Flatiron and begin to climb the switchbacks.
1.5 Arrive at Royal Arch.

The hike: You are going to have to work (and sweat) to get there, but you can savor the views (and alleviate the pain) on the smooth sun-drenched rocks beneath the Royal Arch. This towering red rock structure is as spectacular—and unique—as any of the Flatirons and makes a perfect frame for the views of the plains to the east.

The arch cannot be seen from the trail, which is a good thing because you can use the mystery of the destination as motivation. This is an arduous climb. You will follow steep switchbacks up a forested ravine to a false summit, then wind through rocks and up a creekbed to the arch itself. It is the kind of walking that many adore—full-contact hiking that demands concentration, fortitude, and good hiking shoes.

At the outset, this hike follows the same route as the Bluebell Mesa Loop (Hike 10). Leave the parking lot on the paved Bluebell Canyon Road, which leads south past the charming cottages of Chautauqua Park, then circles west toward the Flatirons. At the Mesa Trail crossing at 0.4 mile, stay right (southwest) on the road; stay left (still southwest) at the Bluebell Shelter sign.

At 0.5 mile, you will reach the Royal Arch Trailhead, marked by a yellow sign indicating that this hike is of moderate difficulty. Pass the picnic area as you turn left (south) onto the trail and walk into the cool woods. The trail drops into and out of a gully, then crosses a seasonal stream and heads up the west-facing side of the gully. The Third Flatiron rises to the west, across the gully, at about 0.8 mile.

Climb eleven—count 'em, eleven—steep switchbacks to the ridgetop at about the 1-mile mark. This is a nice place to take a break, with sun-warmed rocks and views east onto the high plains. From the ridgetop, the trail descends steeply to a saddle. Drop down to the southeast on the trail, which heads up again, this time through a rocky streambed.

A short jaunt over jumbled terrain leads to the arch itself at 1.5 miles, where you can congratulate yourself on a job well done by sprawling on a smooth red slab and enjoying the views.

Descend the way you came. The return is considerably easier (and quicker), since it is downhill most of the way.

Gregory Canyon and Saddle Rock Trails

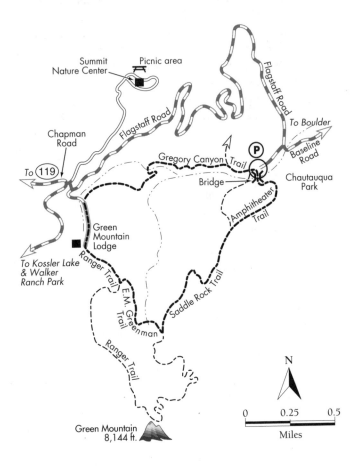

12
GREGORY CANYON AND SADDLE ROCK TRAILS

Type of hike: Loop.
Total distance: 3 miles.
Elevation gain: 900 feet.
Maps: USGS Boulder and Eldorado Springs; Colorado Mountain Club Boulder Group's Trail Map to Boulder Mountain Parks and Nearby Open Space; City of Boulder Open Space & Mountain Parks Lands Trails Map; City of Boulder Circle Hikes pamphlet.
Jurisdiction: City of Boulder Mountain Parks.
Facilities: There is a small parking area, picnic tables, and restrooms at the trailhead. A $3 parking fee is charged for vehicles not registered in Boulder County.
Finding the trailhead: From the intersection of Baseline Road and Broadway, go west up Baseline Road for 1.6 miles, past the entrance to Chautauqua Park, to the base of Flagstaff Mountain. Turn left (southwest) into Gregory Canyon: the trailhead is located beyond the stone bridge.

Key points:
0.0 Trailhead.
1.0 Reach the top of Gregory Canyon.
1.3 Pass the Green Mountain Lodge.
1.5 Reach the E. M. Greenman Trail intersection.
2.0 Begin to descend on the Saddle Rock Trail.

The hike: Climbing into Gregory Canyon, you will be hard-pressed to remember you are on the edge of a major metropolitan area. The trail is wild and rugged from its outset, ascending west along a sun-dappled south-facing slope to the forested apex of a steep ravine. It is not only the stunning scenery that will numb your mind to the civilization that lies to the east; sweat and lactic acid coursing through muscle adds to the enchantment. Lest I have just put you off, remember that any mountain trail is only as hard as you make it. If you keep a pace within your abilities, drink plenty of water, and snack if you need to, this trail is a piece of cake.

And a very rewarding piece at that. As you descend along the Saddle Rock Trail, you will be treated to spectacular views down the canyon and onto the high plains, where the city of Boulder is spread before you like a quilt of silver and gray, stretching to the green and gold of the plains, and melting into the broad blue sky. This trail is also steep, so watch your footing, and take your time.

The trail starts directly west of the parking area, behind the information kiosk and fee station. Within 50 yards, the Saddle Rock Trail breaks off to the left (south). Stay right (west) on the Gregory Canyon Trail, which is marked with a yellow hiker, indicating it as a moderate route.

The path is narrow and rocky, but well kept, climbing amid wildflowers and poison ivy. At about 0.2 mile, pass the Crown Rock Trail, which takes off to the right (north); stay left (west) on the Gregory Canyon Trail.

Cross a small footbridge that spans a drainage as you continue up; a bit higher, the trail passes beneath a rustic power line. You may want to pause and look across the canyon at the rock outcrops that jut out of the forest, but you will need to keep an eye on your footing as you cross slabby sections of the route. A log staircase climbs to a rock staircase that descends to a bridge over a seasonal stream at 0.5 mile. Continue upward, using another log and rock staircase that mitigates an impressive elevation gain.

The trail is mercifully flat for a short distance, but there is more climbing ahead…

As you round a switchback, you will get great views of the sprawling meadows of Chautauqua Park far below. A second switchback follows, then more stair-step climbing over mildly exposed slabs. Above is the shade of evergreens; the trail switchbacks through this shade at the head of the canyon. At about 1 mile, you can hear traffic on Flagstaff Road, and —oh, be joyful—the worst of the climbing is past.

The trail meanders southwest through a small meadow, crossing a little seasonal stream, and merges with a service road that leads south to the Ranger and E. M. Greenman Trails. At 1.3 miles, you will arrive at the old Green Mountain Lodge, where you will find restrooms, picnic tables, and a trail sign. The Ranger Trail is to the east of the quaint and rustic building.

The Ranger Trail arcs southeast from the lodge into tall evergreens, climbing up a flight of log steps to the intersection with the E. M. Greenman trail at 1.5 miles (the trail sign reads H. L. Greenman). Go left (northeast) on the Greenman Trail, which traverses the forested east face of Green Mountain, then winds through a lush gully full of ferns and wild berries nurtured by a small stream. There are many sensitive plant species growing along this route, so please stay on the trail. Another set of rustic stairs leads up to the intersection of Saddle Rock and Greenman Trails. Go left (northeast) on the Saddle Rock Trail at the 2-mile mark.

A brief climb over jumbled rock leads to lovely views west and north of the high peaks and rolling foothills. As the trail traverses the mountainside the views only get better, ultimately opening eastward over the Boulder Valley and high plains. This is the perfect place to park yourself on a rock and enjoy; you've surely earned it!

From its high point, the Saddle Rock Trail plunges steeply down, back into Gregory Canyon. The route is rocky in sections, once again following staircases and switchbacks. Take the time, however, to pause at viewpoints and enjoy more vistas of the plains and the Flatirons; they soon will be lost in the trees.

Pass a climbing access trail at about 2.3 miles; stay left (down and north) on the Saddle Rock Trail. The trail follows a wooden walkway into a fern-filled gully, then parallels a red rock slab and passes a jumble of rocks that serves as yet another overlook. The trail curves right (east) around the base of the slab.

At about 2.5 miles, you will reach the intersection of the Saddle Rock and Amphitheater Trails. You can follow either, but to get views of rock climbers, go right (northeast) on the Amphitheater Trail. Stairs break up this descent too; as you drop, you will pass the red rocks that climbers love. It is a short hop to the trailhead from the overhanging rocks; climb down the stairs to the bridge that spans the creek at the Gregory Canyon Trailhead.

13
UTE AND RANGE VIEW TRAILS

Type of hike: Loop.
Total distance: 1 mile.
Elevation gain: 140 feet.
Maps: USGS Boulder and Eldorado Springs; Colorado Mountain Club Boulder Group's Trail Map to Boulder Mountain Parks and Nearby Open Space; City of Boulder Open Space & Mountain Parks Lands Trails Map.
Jurisdiction: City of Boulder Mountain Parks.
Facilities: In addition to parking, there are restrooms and picnic facilities at the trailhead. A $3 parking fee is charged for vehicles not registered in Boulder County.
Finding the trailhead: Drive west on Baseline Road from its intersection with Broadway for 1.3 miles, past the entrance to Chautauqua Park, to where it merges with the Flagstaff Road. Follow this busy, scenic road for 3.4 miles to the parking area at Realization Point. The gated road/trail to the summit of Flagstaff Mountain begins here as well.

Key points:
0.0 Trailhead.
0.4 Reach the Range View trail intersection.
0.7 Pass the vista point.

Ute and Range View Trails

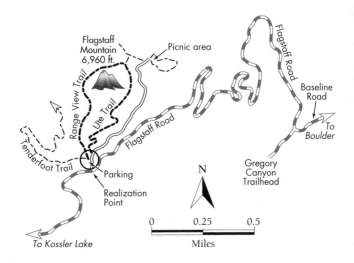

The hike: This easy, well-maintained path, which circles the summit of Flagstaff Mountain, one of Boulder's landmarks, offers a look at the complex urban and wildland interface. From the east side of Flagstaff Mountain, the panorama of the high plains, painted with the sprawling handiwork of humankind, spreads to the horizon. Views on the west side of the mountain are of the snowy Indian Peaks and of the steep forested mountains that rise before them. The juxtaposition is thought-provoking, and this trail is the perfect venue for contemplation of the implications.

This is an ideal hike for children as well as the philosophical, because it is not that difficult, the views are spectacular, and the flora, fauna, and geology of the area are described on interpretive signs along the trail.

The green Ute Trail sign is located just uphill (north) from the gate. Climb the trail through meadow and ponderosa; you can glimpse the plains and the back side of the Flatirons through the trees. The trail loops through the meadow via an elongated "S" curve, then passes through a jumble of logs and rocks as it bends back to the east and flattens.

Ramble though a ponderosa parkland, then begin a slight descent, passing an interpretive sign and several trail markers, to the Range View trail intersection at about 0.4 mile. The Ute Trail continues right (northeast) to picnic shelters. Go left (west) and up on the Range View Trail, passing another interpretive sign.

The Range View Trail climbs up through the dense woods on the northwest face of Flagstaff Mountain. Breaks in the woods offer you the chance to enjoy stunning views west of the Indian Peaks. The trail begins to descend, then passes a rock outcrop that offers a wonderful opportunity to enjoy the western panorama.

At about 0.7 mile, you will pass another vista point and begin down a rustic stairway. Four switchbacks drop you down a semi-exposed slope into the trees. Pass a field of glacial boulders, then continue through the woods to the trailhead and parking area.

Meyers Homestead Trail

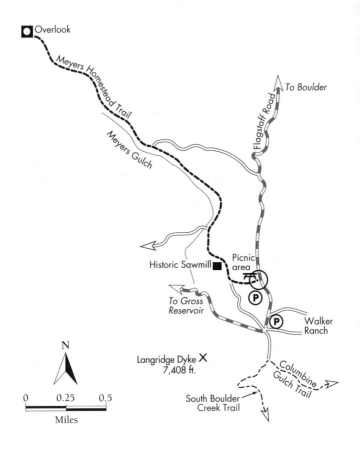

□ Overlook

Meyers Homestead Trail

Meyers Gulch

To Boulder

Flagstaff Road

Historic Sawmill ■

Picnic area

Ⓟ

To Gross Reservoir

Ⓟ

Walker Ranch

N

Langridge Dyke ✕
7,408 ft.

Columbine Gulch Trail

South Boulder Creek Trail

0   0.25   0.5
Miles

14
MEYERS HOMESTEAD TRAIL

Type of hike: Out-and-back.
Total distance: About 5 miles.
Elevation gain: 560 feet.
Maps: USGS Eldorado Springs; City of Boulder Open Space & Mountain Parks Trails Map; Walker Ranch Park brochure.
Jurisdiction: Boulder County Parks and Open Space.
Facilities: In addition to parking, there are picnic sites at the trailhead.
Finding the trailhead: From the intersection of Baseline Road and Broadway, drive west on Baseline Road for 1.3 miles, past the entrance to Chautauqua Park, to where it merges with Flagstaff Road. Follow Flagstaff Road for 7.3 miles, climbing over the shoulder of Flagstaff Mountain, to the parking area, which is on the west side of the pavement and is well marked.

Key points:
0.0 Trailhead.
2.5 Reach the head of the meadow and the overlook.

The hike: To have homesteaded in this rugged high-country valley would have taken more energy and dedication than most hikers traveling the Meyers Homestead Trail today could ever muster. But the broad, green meadows, thick aspen glens, and the clear waters of South Boulder Creek and its tributaries evoke the same passion for the wilderness those hardy pioneers must have felt.

This is a wide, gently ascending trail that is shared by hikers, horseback riders, and mountain bikers. At trail's end, a soft blanket of grass and wildflowers spreads up to a rocky saddle. Vistas of the white peaks of the Continental Divide stretching west from this outcrop will make you wish you could live here too.

Depart from the west end of the parking lot on the abandoned road that now serves as the Meyers Homestead Trail, and begin a gentle descent. After less than 0.1 mile, you will pass a trail marker; an old sawmill sits in the meadow below and west of the trail. The trail then follows the stream that waters the gulch as it begins to climb.

The path is like a roller coaster (but one that mostly ascends). At about the 1-mile mark, crest a hill, descend briefly, then continue up along the stream. Another trail marker is located midway up the next hill.

The trail climbs through a small meadow, then into an aspen grove, at about 2 miles. Pass a trail sign, crest another hill, and begin another short descent. At about 2.5 miles, you will climb into the gorgeous meadow near the trail's end, passing yet another trail marker.

At the head of the meadow, the trail curves west into rocks and trees. From trail's end, you can see past the bare cone of Sugarloaf Mountain to the Indian Peaks, and north to the stately slopes of Longs Peak.

After you contemplate the scenery, leave the saddle and follow the same trail back to the trailhead. The land beyond the trail's end is private; please do not trespass.

15
MOUNT SANITAS AND MOUNT SANITAS VALLEY TRAILS

Type of hike: Loop.
Total distance: 3.1 miles.
Elevation gain: 1200 feet.
Maps: USGS Boulder; City of Boulder Open Space & Mountain Parks Lands Trails Map; Colorado Mountain Club Boulder Group's Trail Map to Boulder Mountain Parks and Nearby Open Space; Mount Sanitas brochure.
Jurisdiction: City of Boulder Open Space Department.
Facilities: There is a small parking area and picnic facilities at the trailhead.
Finding the trailhead: From the intersection of Baseline Road and Broadway, follow Broadway north for 1.8 miles to Mapleton Avenue. Go left (west) on Mapleton Avenue for 0.8 miles, passing the old hospital, to the parking area on the north side of the road at the mouth of Sunshine Canyon.

Key points:
0.0 Trailhead.
0.5 Climb onto the ridge.
1.3 Reach the summit.
2.0 Meet the Mount Sanitas Valley Trail.

The hike: Undoubtedly one of the longest and most strenuous hikes in this book, Mount Sanitas is also one of the

Mount Sanitas and
Mount Sanitas Valley Trails

6,979 ft.

Local access

Local access

Mount
Sanitas
6,863 ft.

East Ridge Trail

Mount Sanitas Trail

Mount Sanitas Valley Trail

Dakota Ridge Trail

To 36

Sunshine Canyon

Broadway

P ■ Mapleton Avenue

N

0   0.25   0.5
Miles

To 93

most rewarding. The trail to the top of the rolling peak is challenging; the rocky, sparsely forested terrain commands a hiker's attention. But so do the great views! The plains stretch away to the east, and the white-capped Indian Peaks rise to the west; the vistas are infinitely rewarding.

The descent from the forested summit is tricky in spots, but the rock formations (and modern rock art) along the path are pleasant diversions. And in the Mount Sanitas Valley, at the foot of the mountain, the hike finishes with a peaceful stroll through a quiet meadow along a wide trail that is easily shared by hikers, dog walkers, and trail runners.

The loop described here offers access to relative seclusion just minutes from downtown Boulder. The rocky spine of the Dakota Hogback, a striking landmark that thrusts skyward repeatedly along Colorado's Front Range, offers more challenging hiking and a chance to watch nimble rock climbers at play.

Timing this hike is difficult: If you try to keep up with the aerobic animals who run the trail, you could do it in an hour. Most will choose a more leisurely pace, and if properly coaxed, even a young child can climb this friendly mountain.

To begin the loop, walk past the picnic shelter at the trailhead, cross a footbridge, and head left (northwest) on the stair-step trail. After ascending a second flight of stairs, you will cross another footbridge. Above the third staircase, you will pass rock-climbing areas on the right (east). A spur trail goes off to the left (west); stay straight on the main route.

At a notch at about the 0.5-mile mark, the trail crosses to the east side of the ridge, offering views of the Sanitas Valley below, as well as the high plains beyond. The trail crosses the ridgeline repeatedly as it ascends over the next mile, offering alternating views west to the Continental Divide and east toward the plains. At 1.3 miles, you will enter a wooded area as the trail curves back to the east—at this point, the top is in sight!

After a rest on the summit rocks, you will leave the peak via the steep, switchbacking East Ridge Trail, which dives eastward into the Sanitas Valley. On the steep, rocky descent, you will pass a striking rock grotto decorated with a stylized painting of an eagle, then, near the base of the mountain, a historical marker. Continue down on the main trail, descending switchbacks to the valley floor.

At about 2 miles, you will meet the wide Mount Sanitas Valley Trail. Pass the two footpaths breaking off to the left (north and east) that provide access to local residents, remaining on the broad swath that heads south through the wide, gentle, grass-cloaked valley. You will pass four intersections with the Dakota Ridge Trail, which serves as a wild barrier between the parkland and a quiet Boulder neighborhood, as the Mount Sanitas Valley Trail descends to the bridge and shelter at the trailhead (3.1 miles).

Option: If you choose, you can follow the Dakota Ridge Trail back to the trailhead. Pick up the trail near the northern end of the Mount Sanitas Valley, where the East Ridge Trail intersects the Mount Sanitas Valley Trail, and follow the rocky ridge south to the trailhead. You can also make an easy 2.1-mile loop of the Mount Sanitas Valley Trail and Dakota Ridge Trail, which is perfect for a late afternoon walk.

16
CANYON LOOP TRAIL

Type of hike: Loop.
Total distance: 3.2 miles.
Elevation gain: 600 feet.
Maps: USGS Boulder; City of Boulder Open Space & Mountain Parks Lands Trails Map; Colorado Mountain Club Boulder Group's Trail Map to Boulder Mountain Parks and Nearby Open Space; Betasso Preserve brochure.
Jurisdiction: Betasso Preserve, Boulder County Parks and Open Space.
Facilities: There are restrooms, picnic tables, and parking at the trailhead. Additional parking is available 0.2 mile east of the preserve's main entrance.
Finding the trailhead: From the intersection of Baseline Road and Broadway, take Broadway north for 1.5 miles to Canyon Boulevard (Colorado 119). Go left (west) on CO 119, into Boulder Canyon, traveling 5.3 miles to Sugarloaf Road. Turn right (north), and follow Sugarloaf Road for 0.9 mile to Betasso Road. Take a right (east) turn on Betasso Road, and follow it for 0.5 mile to an open gate on the left (north). Go through the gate, and follow the preserve road for 0.1 mile to the Canyon Loop Trail parking area. The gate may be closed in winter.

Canyon Loop Trail

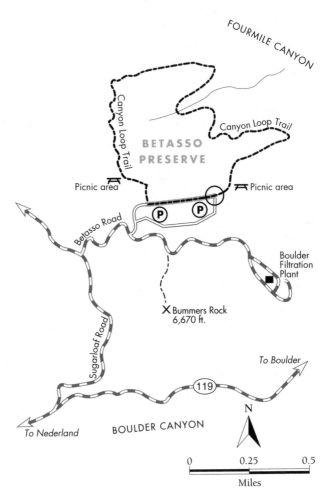

Key points:
0.0 Trailhead.
0.4 Pass the first trail marker.
1.0 Pass the second trail marker.
2.0 Climb onto the crest of a ridge.

The hike: If Grandma's House were at trail's end, this would be a fairy-tale "through the woods" experience. And nary a big bad wolf in sight…

The Canyon Loop Trail weaves through the expansive Betasso Preserve, more than 700 acres of open meadows and forested ravines between Fourmile Canyon and Boulder Canyon. This wonderful path, which offers hikers the opportunity to enjoy great views, an abundance of wildlife, and the potential for solitude, is a singular experience that should not be missed.

The Betasso Preserve is adjacent to the site of a once-busy milling and mining hub called Orodell. No sign of this long-defunct town lies along the Canyon Loop Trail; instead of visiting the relics of history, you will wander in and out of densely wooded ravines that stretch from the mountains east toward the high plains. About half the trail passes through thick Douglas-fir on north-facing slopes; this forest is host to sparse but gorgeous wildflowers in spring. Much of the rest of the trail is shaded by vanilla-scented ponderosa pines and striking Rocky Mountain junipers, which grow above a carpet of lush grass and flowers.

The trail, which was rerouted in late 1999, is narrow single-track, making it difficult at times to pass other trail users. The route also gets heavy mountain bike traffic in the evening hours.

The trailhead is near the northeast corner of the preserve's access road; from here, the trail leads north and up on an old service road into a stand of tall ponderosa. Pass a group picnic area at the top of the hill, then head down through a gate, passing an informational sign.

The trail begins as a roller coaster might, climbing and descending the shoulders of narrow ridges as it rambles north and east through the ravines. You will pass a couple of trail markers as you hike, the first at about 0.4 mile, the second at about 1 mile, on the top of a hill from which views stretch east to the high plains. Head east, climb onto a little knoll, then begin to descend.

At about 1.5 miles, the trail circles a knob, from which there are wonderful views, and then winds west along a south-facing slope. Hike through another ravine; the trail hooks back east into the woods, then around switchbacks through several gullies.

Climb onto the crest of a ridge at about the 2-mile mark. The trail continues gently up and south to an intersection with an unmarked footpath. Stay south on the Canyon Loop Trail, which reenters the wooded parkland of junipers.

At the next intersection, bypass the unmarked spur trail and continue south, passing the picnic area and dropping down onto the preserve road, which leads back to the trailhead parking area.

17
SUGARLOAF MOUNTAIN

Type of hike: Out-and-back.
Total distance: About 2 miles.
Elevation gain: 477 feet.
Topo map: USGS Gold Hill.
Jurisdiction: Roosevelt National Forest.
Facilities: There is a small parking area at the trailhead.
Finding the trailhead: From the intersection of Baseline Road and Broadway, take Broadway north for 1.5 miles to Canyon Boulevard (Colorado 119). Go left (west) on CO 119 into Boulder Canyon, traveling 5.3 miles to Sugarloaf Road. Follow Sugarloaf Road for 4.9 miles to Sugarloaf Mountain Road (at the top of the hill). Go right (east) on Sugarloaf Mountain Road for 0.8 mile to the parking area for the Sugarloaf and Switzerland Trailheads.

Key points:
0.0 Trailhead.
0.3 Enter the burn zone.
1.0 Reach the summit.

The hike: The top of Sugarloaf Mountain is painfully but exhilaratingly exposed—a jumbled hump of wind-whipped talus that drops away precipitously on all sides. The views will leave you awestruck. The jagged summits of the Indian Peaks rise to the west, and the plains flow endlessly to the

Sugarloaf Mountain

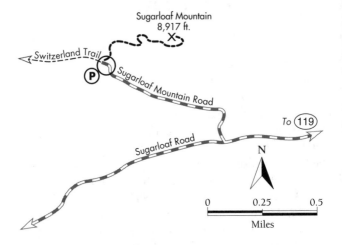

Sugarloaf Mountain
8,917 ft.

Switzerland Trail

Sugarloaf Mountain Road

To (119)

Sugarloaf Road

N

0   0.25   0.5

Miles

east. But the spectacle of devastation born of a recent forest fire is what leaves the biggest impression. Sugarloaf is surrounded by a smattering of homes intermingled with the matchstick-straight and charcoaled remnants of what once was a lush evergreen forest. The fire damage even touches the trail; at one point, you will pass beneath a burled, charred tree trunk that clings tenuously to the mountainside.

Begin the hike on the rugged mining road that climbs from the north end of the parking area (Longs Peak rises dead ahead). The road curves up and eastward. Don't worry about any forks in the route—all paths merge again within the first 0.1 mile of the hike.

Three switchbacks lead up the west face of Sugarloaf Mountain, passing through a sparse forest carpeted with verdant kinnikinnick and small, low-growing wildflowers. Views to the west are of the stark Continental Divide.

At about 0.3 mile, as you traverse the mountain's western face, you will enter the stark burn zone. Talus spreads uphill and down from the path; as you climb the exposed slope, you will pass beneath the gnarled, charred remains of an evergreen tree.

The route circles the south face of Sugarloaf, with views east of the plains. At the next switchback, the flatland vistas give way to a snowcapped panorama. And when you reach the rocky summit plateau, at 1 mile, you can survey 360 degrees of beauty and destruction. The few fire pits amidst the talus are solemn reminders of the power that transformed the nearby landscape.

You will descend via the same route. Though it is all downhill, the walking is tricky, especially since your eyes are often drawn from the trail to the views. Watch your step as you retreat to the car.

White Rocks Section of the East Boulder Trail

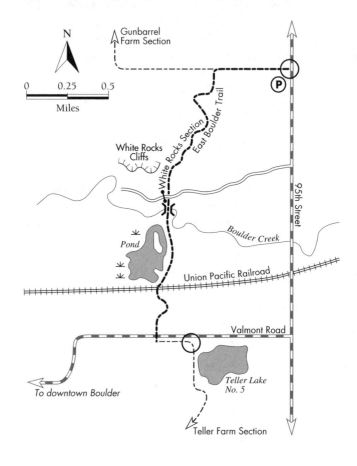

N

0   0.25   0.5

Miles

Gunbarrel Farm Section

P

White Rocks Cliffs

White Rocks Section

East Boulder Trail

95th Street

Pond

Boulder Creek

Union Pacific Railroad

Valmont Road

To downtown Boulder

Teller Lake No. 5

Teller Farm Section

18

WHITE ROCKS SECTION OF THE EAST BOULDER TRAIL

Type of hike: Out-and-back.
Total distance: 4.4 miles.
Elevation gain: 80 feet.
Maps: USGS Niwot; City of Boulder Open Space & Mountain Parks Lands Trails Map.
Jurisdiction: City of Boulder Open Space Department.
Facilities: There is parking at the trailhead, but no restroom or picnic facilities. No dogs are permitted on this section of the trail. Please remain on the designated trail.
Finding the trailhead: From the intersection of Baseline Road and Broadway, go east on Baseline Road for 0.4 mile to U.S. Highway 36, also known as 28th Street. Go left (north) on US 36 for 2 miles to Valmont Road. Turn right (east) on Valmont Road, and follow Valmont for 1.1 miles to a right (south) turn to the intersection of Pearl Street and 55th Street. Turn left (east) onto Pearl (Valmont), and continue east for a total of 5.4 miles to the intersection of Valmont and 95th Street. Go left (north) on 95th Street for 1.5 miles to West Phillips Road; there is a brown City of Boulder Open Space sign on the left (west) side of the road. Turn left (west) on West Phillips into the parking area.

Key points:

0.0 Trailhead.
0.5 Pass the start of the Gunbarrel Farm Section of the trail.

1.0 Pass views of the White Rocks.
1.5 Skirt the ponds.

The hike: There is a quandary on the plains east of Boulder, and the unsuspecting hiker will be hard-pressed to resolve it. Is the vision that rises to the west, of foothills and Flatirons and the snowy peaks of the Continental Divide, the highlight of the White Rocks Section of the East Boulder Trail? Or is it the chalky cliffs of the White Rocks, exposed from the grassy monotony of the high plains by Boulder Creek to become the home of raptors and songbirds? Or is it meandering Boulder Creek, shadowed by cottonwoods and elms and wearing a lacy glove of wildflowers? No need to fret—better to just enjoy all the sights in all their glory.

The White Rocks that give this portion of the trail its name are sandstone cliffs formed 70 million years ago when the plains were an inland sea. Their formation is explained on one of several interpretive signs that line the trail.

The route begins to the west of the parking area, heading west on a doubletrack path between fences, with houses on the right (north) and the mountains brilliant on the horizon. At 0.5 mile, reach the trail intersection between the White Rocks Section and the Gunbarrel Farm Section of the East Boulder Trail. The trail to Gunbarrel Farm goes straight (west). Instead, turn left (south), across the paved private drive and past the "Welcome to White Rocks" sign.

The trail, which is shared with horseback riders and mountain bikers, rolls through swales as it heads down the prairie. Bluebirds and butterflies light in the grasses, and opulent homes are perched on high points. Trail signs keep you on track as you slide through a drainage; beyond, the trail jogs west, then south toward pastures and ponds.

Near the bottom of the mesa at about 1 mile, pass an interpretive sign and views of the White Rocks. The trail narrows, crosses a bridge over a draw, and enters the riparian zone along Boulder Creek. A culvert and bridge span Boulder Creek; pause here, and watch the sparkling water flow east.

South of Boulder Creek, at about 1.5 miles, interpretive signs describe the reclamation of the gravel pits and the wildlife that inhabit the resulting ponds. The bird life is abundant and spectacular, changing with seasonal migrations of cranes, geese, raptors, and songbirds. Continue south along the trail, which widens again and is shaded by rustling cottonwoods. At about 2 miles, cross the Union Pacific Railroad tracks; the trail briefly parallels the tracks heading east before arcing south again. Pass between pastures and farm buildings. At a westward bend in the trail, pass another welcome sign; the path parallels a ditch to its end at Valmont Road.

Return as you came, enjoying different and wonderful views of the White Rocks and the foothills as you climb back to the trailhead.

Options: There are two other sections of the East Boulder Trail that invite exploration. The Teller Farm Section begins across Valmont Road, about 0.2 mile east (left) of the south end of the White Rocks Section. The Gunbarrel Farm Section can be reached from the trailhead on West Phillips Road, and heads west when the White Rocks Section breaks to the south.

19
WALDEN AND SAWHILL PONDS

Type of hike: Loop.
Total distance: 2.75 miles.
Elevation gain: Minimal.
Maps: USGS Niwot; City of Boulder Open Space & Mountain Parks Lands Trails Map.
Jurisdiction: Boulder County Parks and Open Space, and City of Boulder Mountain Parks.
Facilities: In addition to ample parking, there are restrooms and picnic areas at the trailhead.
Finding the trailhead: From the intersection of Baseline Road and Broadway, go east on Baseline Road for 0.4 mile to U.S. Highway 36, also known as 28th Street. Go left (north) on US 36 for 2 miles to Valmont Road. Turn right (east) on Valmont Road, and follow Valmont for 4.4 miles to 75th Street. Turn left (north) on 75th Street and go 0.8 mile to the Walden Ponds park access road, which is on the left (west) side of the road. Follow the gravel access road for 0.1 mile to the parking area at Picnic Pond, where there is access for persons with disabilities, or for 0.4 mile to the main parking lot and trailhead at Cottonwood Marsh.

Walden and Sawhill Ponds

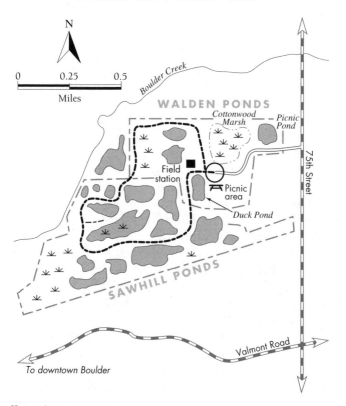

Key points:

0.0 Trailhead.

0.2 Leave the boardwalk.

0.7 Enter the Sawhill Ponds area.

The hike: In a world where it often seems that nature is losing out to development, the Walden Wildlife Habitat and Sawhill Ponds are a refreshing confirmation that sometimes the opposite is the case.

Not only have the ponds a distinctly urban setting, they were born of progress. The gravel that makes up the sediments along the Boulder Creek drainage, in which the ponds sit, was once mined extensively for use in road building. When the gravel mine began its long journey back to a more natural state—in the case of Walden Ponds, as a result of a reclamation project initiated by Boulder County in 1974—ponds and islands were sculpted of the remaining mined rock. Rain and meltwater filled the depressions, trees and shrubs were planted... and before long, a wildlife habitat capable of supporting a variety of bird, fish, insect, and mammal species had taken shape where once there was only rubble.

This hike links trails through both the Walden Ponds Wildlife Habitat area, managed by Boulder County Parks and Open Space, and the Sawhill Ponds area, managed by the City of Boulder Mountain Parks. A number of spur trails exist in the Sawhill Ponds area; this route follows the main doubletrack trail (an old roadbed), which features interesting interpretive signs.

Begin the hike at the left (west) end of the main parking lot on the Cottonwood Marsh Trail, and follow the boardwalk along the edge of the water through cattails and past overlook points outfitted with interpretive signs.

At the end of the boardwalk, at about 0.2 mile, go left (northwest) on the broad gravel trail. At the road leading to the park's field station, go left (northwest) to the north side of the buildings, and pick up the trail. Pass Bass Pond, which is on your left (west) as you walk northward.

At the northeast corner of Bass Pond, a spur trail leads north to a neighborhood street. Stay left (west), circling the pond. At the northwest corner of the pond, at about 0.5 mile, the wide gravel track disintegrates to weedy double-track, and circles Pelican Marsh.

At the southwest corner of Pelican Marsh, at about 0.7 mile, enter the Sawhill Ponds area. Go left (west) on the gravel road, and stay right (straight/west) where a spur trail veers off to the left (south). The Sawhill Ponds are much wilder than the Walden Ponds, with thick vegetation growing both along the shores of the ponds and within the water. At the third pond, with a thick marsh crowding its west end, follow the old roadbed as it circles to the south.

At about 1.5 miles, the route curves left (east) where another nameless spur trail intersects. Pass an interpretive sign that discusses the dragonfly; you will be glad to learn these iridescent creatures feed on mosquitoes. Continue east to a second interpretive sign, which describes the oldest of the Sawhill Ponds and the reptiles and amphibians that live there.

After passing some side trails leading onto dikes that separate the ponds, you will reach the next major trail intersection at about 2 miles. Veer left (north). The trail splits after about 100 yards; stay right (north). Follow the road along the fenceline, passing another interpretive sign. Walk through an opening in the fence at the Sawhill Ponds entry kiosk, and reenter the Walden Ponds complex near the field station. Turn right (east), cross the field station service road, and retrace your steps across the boardwalk to the trailhead.

20
WONDERLAND LAKE

Type of hike: Loop.
Total distance: 1.7 miles
Elevation gain: Minimal.
Maps: USGS Boulder; City of Boulder Open Space & Mountain Parks Lands Trails Map.
Jurisdiction: City of Boulder Open Space Department.
Facilities: There is ample parking at the trailhead, as well as picnic tables. If it is open, you may also visit the Foothills Nature Center. The trail is accessible to persons with disabilities. Dogs must be on a hand-held leash at all times.
Finding the trailhead: From the intersection of Broadway and Baseline Road, take Broadway north for about 3.3 miles to the Wonderland Lake Trailhead (this is just before Utica Street). The trailhead parking lot is on the left (west) side of the road.

Key points:
0.0 Trailhead.
0.2 Reach Wonderland Lake.
1.2 Pass the Foothills Trail intersection.

The hike: Like that familiar neighborhood stroll, the trail around Wonderland Lake wraps you in ease and comfort. Easy, scenic, and infinitely friendly, this is the perfect choice for a summer evening, when the foothills are backlit by the

Wonderland Lake

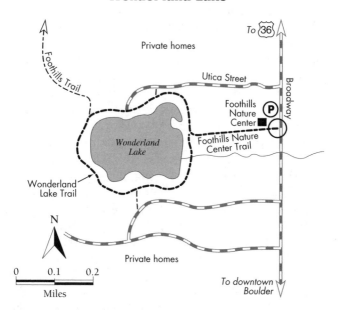

setting sun, and the early morning, when fresh light and dew wash over the lake.

This area is a wildlife sanctuary, offering safe harbor to a variety of species from birds to rattlesnakes, so tread with care. Along the trail's length, you will pass riparian habitat, wetlands, and prairie, which support a great number of flora including colorful wildflowers in late spring and early summer.

To begin, leave the parking lot to the west, past the nature center buildings and trail signs, following the Foothills Nature Center Trail west into the grasslands of a wide greenbelt between two subdivisions. The Dakota Ridge looms to the west. At 0.2 mile, the Foothills Nature Center Trail dead-ends on the Foothills Trail, which bends right (north). Instead, turn left (south) on the Wonderland Lake Trail, walk about 100 feet to the lakeshore, and again bear left (south), passing the Wonderland Lake welcome sign.

The trail leads across the dam; the small lake lies to the west. At 0.5 mile, the trail intersects concrete paths that lead to homes to the south of the lake; you will find manicured lawns, a playground, and benches to rest on at this juncture.

At all the trail junctions along this 0.2-mile stretch of trail, stay right (northwest), curving around the shore of the lake. Pass a trail sign at the southwest corner of the lake, then leave the paved paths behind, and walk north on the gravel track that leads along the lake's west shore. A split-rail fence guards the verdant, birdsong-filled wetland.

Reach a trail intersection at 1.2 miles, on the northwest corner of the lake. Stay right (east) on the Wonderland Lake Trail; the Foothills Trail climbs left (north) and out of the lake's basin. The Wonderland Lake Trail arcs around the north side of the lake. Cross a little footbridge and follow the footpath as it parallels a private driveway. A Wonderland Lake Trail sign points the way. Walk east on the sidewalk bordering Utica Street; after about 150 yards, turn right (south) on the gravel path that leads back to the lake (again, signs indicate the route).

Travel another 150 yards on the gravel path, and you will find yourself back at the intersection with the Foothills Nature Center Trail. From here, retrace your steps to the trailhead.

21
PEAKS TO PINES TRAIL

Type of hike: Loop.
Total distance: 1.25 miles.
Elevation gain: 240 feet.
Maps: USGS Boulder; City of Boulder Open Space & Mountain Parks Lands Trails Map; Colorado Mountain Club Boulder Group's Trail Map to Boulder Mountain Parks and Nearby Open Space; Bald Mountain Scenic Area brochure.
Jurisdiction: Boulder County Parks and Open Space.
Facilities: Parking and picnic sites are available at the trailhead. A portable restroom is on site from May to August.
Finding the trailhead: To reach the Bald Mountain Scenic Area and trailhead from the intersection of Broadway and Baseline Road, follow Broadway north for 1.8 miles to Mapleton Avenue. Go left (west) on Mapleton Avenue for 0.8 mile to the mouth of Sunshine Canyon. Follow the Sunshine Canyon Road for 4.2 miles to the parking lot on the left (south) side of the road.

Key points:
0.0 Trailhead.
0.5 Arrive at the summit.
1.0 Pass a bench offering views of the peaks to the west.

The hike: If male pattern baldness could strike a peak, Bald Mountain would be a textbook case. The ponderosa forest

Peaks to Pines Trail

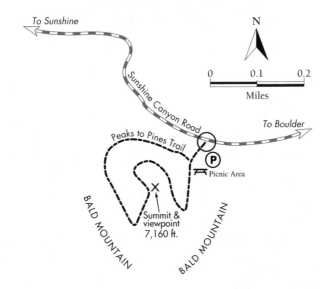

that circles its base is like the fringe of hair that often circles a shiny pate; the few trees that adorn the colorful meadow at the apex of the trail are those last, proud shoots that sometimes sprout from a denuded scalp. Lest the analogy trouble you, this is a remarkable place (as bald men are often remarkable people).

Wind, seasonal weather extremes, and coarse, shallow soil have conspired to make the summit of Bald Mountain a tough place for a forest to take root. This relative lack of fruitfulness has its advantages, however; the views from the summit are among the best in Boulder's back yard, ranging west to the

Indian Peaks, south to the backside of Flagstaff Mountain and the Flatirons, and east to Boulder, Denver, and surrounding plains. A thoughtfully placed bench in the shade of some ponderosa pines is a perfect spot for contemplation.

To begin this short, sweet hike, leave the parking lot and head up the Peaks to Pines Trail, passing the picnic area and over a small footbridge into the ponderosa parkland.

After less than 0.1 mile, round a switchback to a fork in the trail. Go left (northwest) on the path signed "Summit Trail."

Wind through the woods to the western face of the mountain, where you will catch glimpses of the jagged mountains of the Continental Divide through the trees. Climb up to the summit bench at about the 0.5-mile mark, which is sheltered by a smattering of tall ponderosa. The highland meadow spreads around you like a colorful quilt, and the suburbs of the Emerald City (known more commonly as Denver) sparkle on the eastern horizon.

From the summit, head down the grassy south shoulder of the mountain to a lone ponderosa. The trail passes a closed path and circles westward. Pass a footpath that leads to a rock outcrop, then, at 1 mile, a second bench that offers wonderful views of the saw-toothed peaks of the Continental Divide.

The trail circles back to the east face of Bald Mountain and the Summit Trail crossing. Continue down on the Peaks to Pines Trail, which leads back through the picnic area to the parking lot.

Boulder Valley Ranch Loop

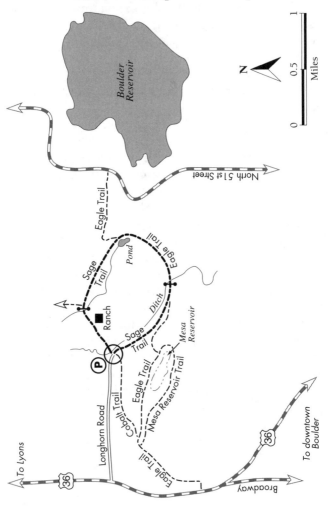

22
BOULDER VALLEY RANCH LOOP

Type of hike: Loop.
Total distance: 2.8 miles.
Elevation gain: 100 feet.
Maps: USGS Boulder; City of Boulder Open Space & Mountain Parks Lands Trails Map.
Jurisdiction: City of Boulder Open Space Department.
Facilities: There is plenty of parking and restrooms at the trailhead.
Finding the trailhead: To reach Boulder Valley Ranch from the intersection of Broadway and Baseline Road, take Broadway north for 4.3 miles to where it ends at U.S. Highway 36. Go left (north) on US 36 for 1.1 miles, and turn right (east) on Longhorn Road. Follow Longhorn Road, which begins as pavement and becomes a well-maintained gravel road after 0.2 mile, for a total of 1 mile to the trailhead parking area, which is on the right (south) side of the road.

Key points:
0.0 Trailhead.
0.7 Reach the intersection with the Eagle Trail.
1.8 Pass the pond and reach the Sage Trail.
2.7 Skirt the ranch buildings as you head back to the trailhead.

The hike: When you think of Boulder, no doubt mountains spring to mind, but the fact of the matter is, the city lies mostly on the flats—flats that are every bit as beautiful as the highlands but in a very different way.

Though civilization encroaches on portions of this hike, when you drop into the draw near the pond at the loop's eastern end, you are embraced by unadulterated high prairie. The grasses wave gold or green, depending on the season, and are thick with wildflowers in late spring and early summer. Birds dip to drink or swim at the pond, and the rounded summits of the foothills line the western horizon. With a bit of luck you will find yourself alone here, and with a bit of imagination, you can transport yourself back to a time when, rather than sprawling suburbia, this was all there was along Colorado's Front Range.

The trail described here links the Sage and Eagle Trails in a relatively flat, easy loop. The path follows a well-maintained roadbed that is used by the rancher who still runs livestock on the property. In addition to domestic animals and prairie dogs, migratory waterfowl and other birds, including raptors, frequent the property.

The hike begins on the Sage Trail, which departs from the south side of the parking area. The Cobalt Trail takes off to the west from the trailhead as well; stay straight (south) on the Sage Trail.

Tall grass and yucca line the west side of the trail; blowsy cottonwoods drink from the ditch that runs along the east side of the path. The route slowly veers southeast, wedged between the low, scrub-covered ridge and the ditch. To the east, the green and rust-colored stain of wetlands spills

82

through the grasses toward the Boulder Reservoir, which lies to the east of the park.

At 0.7 mile, the Sage Trail ends at the Eagle Trail. Pass the gate and cross the ditch to the intersection with the Eagle Trail. The Eagle Trail goes both right and left at this point; continue left (east and north) on the trail (the right fork climbs west toward the foothills). The trail swings north, and curves into the waist-deep prairie grasses; at 1.2 miles, in the thick of the grassland, you will pass an "Eagle Trail" sign and drop toward the pond. In the bottom of the shallow bowl, on the pond's dam, you can envision yourself in the belly of the fabled American West—for as long as the bugs that flourish in the pungent marsh allow you to linger.

Cross the dam; on its north side, a sign points you north, up the road, to the trail intersection with the Sage Trail at 1.8 miles. Turn left (west) on the Sage Trail; the Eagle Trail continues east to 55th Street, which can be followed south to the entrance to the Boulder Reservoir.

Walk west along the ranch road toward the foothills for almost 0.5 mile to a gate, where the North Rim Trail takes off to the right (north), leading to nearby subdivisions. Continue west, passing the gate and walking through another buggy marsh. When you reach the clustered ranch buildings, stay right (north), passing through another gate on the northern boundary of the ranch complex. Continue southwest on the trail beyond the ranch, which climbs back to the trailhead parking area at 2.7 miles.

Although dogs on these trails are only required to be under voice and sight control, be considerate of other trail users, and keep your dog nearby or on a leash at all times.

Little Thompson Overlook Trail

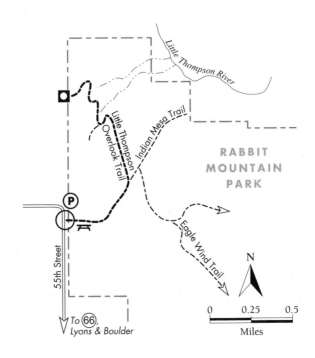

23
LITTLE THOMPSON OVERLOOK TRAIL

Type of hike: Out-and-back.
Total distance: 2 miles.
Elevation gain: 500 feet.
Maps: USGS Lyons; Rabbit Mountain Open Space brochure.
Jurisdiction: Boulder County Parks and Open Space.
Facilities: There is a large parking lot, as well as restrooms and picnic areas, at the trailhead.
Finding the trailhead: From the intersection of Broadway and Baseline Road, take Broadway north for 4.3 miles to where it ends at U.S. Highway 36. Go left (north) on US 36 for 10.5 miles to its intersection with Colorado 66. Turn right (east) on CO 66, and go 1 mile to North 53rd Street; there is a Rabbit Mountain Open Space sign preceding the turn-off. Go left (north) on North 53rd Street, a good gravel road that becomes North 55th Street, for 2.8 miles to the trailhead parking area.

Key points:
0.0 Trailhead.
0.5 Reach the main trail intersection.
1.0 Arrive at the Little Thompson Overlook.

The hike: Rabbit Mountain whispers of the wild west. It is raw and scrubby and drenched in sunshine, inviting and aloof, plain and starkly beautiful. Once the winter refuge of Arapaho Indians, it now welcomes hikers and mountain bikers seeking a solitude that can only be found outside of the city—even an outdoorsy city like Boulder.

The park straddles the interface between the high plains and the mountains, and while its steepness is born of the high country, the dry, high-desert scrub that dominates the flora along the Little Thompson Overlook Trail gives it more of a lowland feel. The overlook itself offers views down into the canyon carved by the Little Thompson River, and across the high plains to the north and east; on the return journey, the views are of the Front Range stretching away to the south, and occasional glimpses of the snowy peaks of the Continental Divide to the west.

Watch for raptors overhead; the trails are subject to seasonal closures between February 1 and July 31 to protect nesting birds. Also, be aware that rattlesnakes are common here; they generally avoid contact with humans, and will only strike if cornered or threatened.

The hike begins northeast of the information kiosk, climbing gently along a rocky trail that traverses the south-facing slope, with the old roadbed that serves as the Indian Mesa Trail below and to the right (south). In summer, crickets are thick along the footpath, and hurl themselves clear of hiking boots like Mexican jumping beans. Climb two switchbacks, passing a trail sign where the old roadbed joins the footpath, to the main trail intersection at 0.5 mile. At this point, the Indian Mesa Trail continues northeast, and offers access to the Eagle Wind Trail, which heads southeast. Turn left (northwest) on the Little Thompson Overlook Trail.

After a brief flat traverse through a sparse meadow, a trail sign points you up and northwest on the rocky route. It is a steady climb to another trail sign indicating that the overlook trail goes right (west) and down. The spur trail to the left (southwest) is unnamed.

Follow the Little Thompson Overlook Trail down through a low-growing, silvery sea of yucca, mountain mahogany, and prickly pear, occasionally passing a fragrant juniper or a cluster of wildflowers. The trail traverses through three gullies as it winds out to the overlook; the first is the deepest, the second holds two rocky "bridges" over the seasonal drainage, and the third is very shallow. Beyond the last gully, the trail ends on a rocky point at 1 mile. From here, you can gaze north into the milky-walled canyon threaded by the Little Thompson River. The bleached, striated walls of the Dakota Ridge, also known as the Dakota Hogback, arch skyward above the river basin. The sight is truly sublime.

To return, retrace your steps to the trailhead, enjoying a different set of wonderful views as you descend.

Options: If you'd like to sample more of Rabbit Mountain's wildness, you can follow the Eagle Wind Trail out to the southeast, or circle back to the trailhead via the broad Indian Mesa Trail.